Historic Images of
HAVELOCK
& CHERRY POINT

A Photographic Tour
of the Community's Past

EDWARD BARNES ELLIS, JR.

McBryde Publishing

NEW BERN, NORTH CAROLINA USA

Historic Images of Havelock and Cherry Point

Published by McBryde Publishing, Inc.
New Bern, North Carolina, USA

Printed in the United States of America

ISBN: 978-0-9843184-1-4

Cover Design: Bill Benners
Book Layout: Shannon Richards

First Edition
January, 2010

THE GOOD LIFE—Could they be happier? Two men play cards at a handmade table in this emblematic photo of life in a time gone by. With both guns and liquor at the ready, the pair looks as if they have not a care in the world. Today, we would bring unwieldy folding chairs to the woods, but these fellows relax in bent-wood rockers.

In memory of my parents,
Ed and Janice Ellis

ALSO BY THE AUTHOR

In This Small Place:
Amazing Tales of the First 300 Years
of Havelock and Craven County, North Carolina

New Bern History 101:
The Essential Facts for the Native, Newcomer
or Visitor to the Colonial Capital of North Carolina

RARE IMAGE—This is the only photograph known to exist of Trader's Store before it was moved in the 1920s across the road to its current location on Miller Boulevard. The photo shows women and girls on a porch that was removed when the building was lifted from its foundation and, according to local word-of-mouth, rolled on logs cross what was then the Beaufort Road. Since the ends of the old country store are identical, it is possible that the front became the back, and vice versa, simplifying the relocation of a structure that has become a local icon of history. Here, black and white children sit, stand and play as two adult females on the steps look at the camera in this never-before-published image believed to date from 1923.

CONTENTS

TRAINING HOP—The crews of PBJ 1-D Mitchell Bombers of Cherry Point's Marine Bomber Squadron 613, including MB-3 shown here, flew training missions over eastern North Carolina during the summer of 1944 in preparation for World War II Pacific combat. Among other places, the squadron's fifteen aircraft saw service in the Caroline Islands, Saipan and Iwo Jima. With a cruising speed of 230 mph and a crew of seven, missions included bombing and strafing Japanese targets, reconnaissance, shipping lane patrols and search and rescue. Like many other aircraft, MB-3 was scrapped at Kwajalein Atoll in the Marshall Islands at war's end.

Introduction

CITIZENS GET FIRED UP

MAIN STREET FURY — When does it begin to dawn on citizens that they need to organize a government? One event stimulating such thoughts was the 1955 fire above. Canipe Buick blazed for several hours across East Main Street from what is today Walter B. Jones Park. This amazing image warrants some analysis. For example, Highway 70 is just two lanes. To the left of the flaming car dealership stands the tallest building ever built in Havelock. The four-story Eastern 5, 10 & 25 Cent Store burst into flames a few minutes after this photograph was made. Both buildings burned to the ground.

The most important thing to notice, however, is not what is in the picture, but what is missing. In twelve photographs known to have been taken during the fire, only one recorded an effort to fight the inferno. Two men in civilian clothes were seen in one frame spraying water with a single hose, but there were no fire trucks, police vehicles or emergency response of any kind.

Whether the Canipe fire was the sole catalyst, 1955 is the year people around Havelock got serious about founding a government. It was a four-year fight … and then some. Through those efforts, the Town of Havelock was successfully incorporated in 1959. But today, more than fifty years after the official founding of the city, it's important to realize and understand that Havelock itself has actually existed much longer.

And a lot has gone on.

The area was settled in the earliest days of America. We know that the Hancock and Slocum families—the namesakes of two of our major local creeks—were here in 1707. That's three years before New Bern was founded. The Hancocks and the Slocums and others may have been here before 1707, but we can prove they were here in that year. We know Havelock took its name more than 150 years ago … in early 1858 upon the completion of the Atlantic & North Carolina railroad between Goldsboro and Beaufort.

In this book, we look back on that time via a "show and tell" featuring a collection of historic images of Havelock and Cherry Point. These have been gleaned from several thousand in the author's Havelock Historical Collection.

We will see old Havelock, old Cherry Point, visit some original families, revisit the establishment of Cherry Point Marine Corps Air Station and greet some of the founders of government and business. And we'll see many places and things that don't exist anymore.

AT EASE—Fun-loving Babe Ruth adored Havelock. He was one of many wealthy and famous people who hunted, fished and blew off steam here in the late 1800s and first part of the 1900s. In this photo taken during a local visit, "The Babe" is casual as can be. Despite his less than Atlas-like physique, and his affinity for strong spirits, tobacco and the chow line, few have approached his success in sports.

Chapter 1

HAVELOCK 1941

VIEW FROM CROSSROADS TO "MAIN GATE"—Of course, in 1941, Cherry Point's main gate did not exist, but today it is at the top of the hill visible in this photograph. The Dick Parker Ford dealership was located to the right in 2010 adjacent to the bridge seen here. The viewer's back is toward the Crossroads created by the modern course of US 70 and its intersection with Miller and Fontana Boulevards. Highway 101, a dirt road, begins where the 1941 path of Highway 70 curves to the right on its course to Newport and Morehead City. Notice the building visible at the road's crest. It's a garage and store owned at the time by Havelock native Frank Russell. In 2010, a real estate company occupied the site. Today, this formerly lonesome stretch of road is one of the busiest thoroughfares in the state. Its four lanes now carry thousands of vehicles each day to and from the Cherry Point Marine Corps Air Station.

A LITTLE FARTHER UP THE ROAD—Looking east on what is today Highway 101. Fontana Blvd., the old two-lane highway bridge across the east prong of Slocum Creek is visible along with the current location of Roosevelt Blvd. at the top of the hill. The Russell store and garage is clearly seen facing the old course of US 70 across the road from the present-day main gate of Cherry Point.

VIEW FROM "MAIN GATE" TOWARD CROSSROADS—The dirt surface of Highway 101/Fontana Blvd. is visible in this 1941 photograph. The location of the "crossroads" is visible, significantly less active at the time than the intersection which handled about fifty thousand cars per day in 2009.

EARLY ENTREPRENEUR— Frank Russell, seen here as a young man, owned the store and garage at the intersection of Highways 70 and 101 across from what is today the Cherry Point main gate. Russell would later operate a diner at the site. One of the diner's charms was Russell's little monkey that was said to swing down on window curtains and scoop a tiny handful of sugar from the dish on a customer's table. We suppose this means the health department was in a rather primitive state at the time. For a while, during the construction of Cherry Point, Russell had the only pay phone for miles around. It was said to have a line twenty-four hours a day.

VIEW DOWN HIGHWAY 101—Today, this is the course of Fontana Blvd. and Highway 101 looking toward Beaufort. The present-day location of Havelock High School would be ahead on the right in this 1941 photograph, one of about a hundred taken under contract for the federal government during the establishment of Cherry Point.

"CHERRY POINT SIX MILES" reads the highway directional sign at left. Although the sign was located near present-day Cherry Point's Gate Six at Cunningham Blvd., it was indeed six miles to Cherry Point proper which at the time was a small settlement on the banks of Hancock Creek near the Neuse River. In horse and buggy days, it took as long for the cousins at Havelock Station to travel to Cherry Point as it takes today to drive from Havelock to Raleigh. A non-powered road grader is visible at left behind the highway sign.

THE CHERRY POINT OFFICERS CLUB today stands on this site on the south bank of the Neuse River occupied by the home of M.T. Bradshaw in 1941. That may be Mr. Bradshaw at right in the photo on land that became subject to condemnation proceedings in preparation for construction of the Cherry Point air station. All the owners of property within the eleven thousand acre proposed base boundary were evicted. Though paid for their land, many said it was not enough to compensate for the value or the disruption of their homes and lives.

G. R. FULLER FISHING CAMP, 1941—Note the fancy water source, a hand pump at the camp on Hancock Creek. The New Bern man who owned the rustic cabin hosted Babe Ruth and other notables there and sometimes acted as a fishing guide. On one boat trip down the Neuse, the propeller struck an object and was sheared off. Fuller rowed the men to shore, built a fire for them and proceeded to whittle a two-blade prop from a block of wood. They got home safely.

G. R. FULLER'S DOCK on Hancock Creek, a tributary of the Neuse which forms the eastern boundary of Cherry Point, was the site of a swimming hole used by local black children. The only problem was that alligators liked to sun themselves there. One of the children, grown well into adulthood, told the author that he and his buddies used to shoo the big creatures away. Asked if he was afraid of them, he laughed and replied that as a kid he was "faster than an alligator."

OCCUPIED HOME AT CHERRY POINT—Taken in August 1941, a blow-up of this photographs reveal two children and a woman hanging clothes behind the home on Slocum Creek. The owners or tenants are unknown as the only record of ownership is in the name of a law firm. The property at Cherry Point fell into three categories: homes, hunting and fishing camps or farms. While homes and camps were white-owned, the farms were almost exclusively African-American.

A SPORTSMEN'S LODGE on Slocum Creek featuring a number of attached dwelling units connected by a long screened porch was a sort of early hunting and fishing motel. This one was owned by R. S. and W. W. Williams. Sportsmen, many of them rich and famous, came from all over the East Coast to enjoy the creeks, river and woodlands around Havelock. Many traveled here by train for a getaway from places like New York City and Philadelphia.

A SLOCUM CREEK CAMP owned by H. H. Hill featuring the first of many hand-built wooden skiffs shown in old local photographs. Boats of all types were the primary form of transportation from colonial times. Small boats were the best way to navigate the area and everyone up until the modern era had one or two. The Hill camp was typical of dozens along the local creek and river.

THE HILL CAMP DOCK with another boat. Other camps and lodges were owned by families and by organizations like the Kinston Fire Department and Durham Police Department. The most famous of all was "Lucky Lodge" on Slocum Creek owned by the American Tobacco Company and the prominent Duke family of Durham. The last three photos mentioned were missing when the Cherry Point collection was discovered in the 1980s.

ONE OF SEVERAL DOZEN FARMS—The eight-acre spread of John Nelson sat near the center of what is today the Marine base at a point where massive runways now intersect. Most of the Cherry Point farms were black–owned and had been for more than a hundred years. While some local families were descendant of slaves freed by the Civil War, others had been free property-owners since the time of the American Revolution.

MARY ANDERSON'S COTTAGE squatted near the intersection of modern Roosevelt Blvd. and Slocum Road. Anderson owned a single acre of quiet seclusion there where she must have enjoyed the covered porch with its view of a pole-mounted bird house. By the time most of the homes were photographed, they had been abandoned for about a year. The disheveled appearance of many of the homes and yards is a result of the long vacancy.

THE TOON FAMILY pictured here is representative of many local residents who lived hand-to-mouth during the Great Depression of the 1930s. Poor families, black and white, led a hard-scrabble existence that relied upon the bounty of the forest and the river ... and whatever could be scratched from the soil. One of the youngsters in the foreground, Albert Toon, would grow up to be a Craven County commissioner.

BE IT EVER SO HUMBLE...—The Michael Toon home place was thirty-one acres at Little Witness, a black hamlet north of Highway 101 on the first big curve on the way to Beaufort. Little Witness was also known as Melvin, N.C. The cluster of homes there shared a church, a school and a cemetery along a network of dirt streets. The family's water source, a hand pump, is visible at bottom left. All of the Little Witness land is today within the fences of Cherry Point.

IN CONTRAST—Ignoring the corn stubble around a home vacant for most of a year, it's easy to see that the Walter Nelson farmhouse was quite substantial. Nelson's large, two-story home boasted double porches—front and side—plus multiple chimneys. The head of a large African-American family, Nelson was one of the most prosperous men in eastern Craven County; a farmer, a businessman and, if local legend is correct, maybe somewhat close to the famous corn "distillation" trade.

A STURDY LOG TOBACCO BARN on Walter Nelson's 130-acre Cherry Point farm has had the metal roofing material carried away for use elsewhere. Many of the residents removed from Cherry Point in the early 1940s salvaged doors, windows, roofing and hardware for use at new residences elsewhere. Most of the black families whose property was condemned moved to the Harlowe area where their descendents still live today.

A BARN, STABLE AND SHOP on the Walter Nelson spread serve as a backdrop for two of his vehicles, a vintage truck and automobile, and give further evidence of Nelson's prosperity in the midst of the Great Depression. Nelson's farm was in a community called "Nelsontown" located in the vicinity of where the departure end of Cherry Point Runway 32 Right opens onto Roosevelt Boulevard today.

TWO MORE NELSON BARNS—These two tobacco barns are built in an older style with round logs, the same type of construction used in pioneer cabins. Gaps between the logs were chinked with mud to hold in the hot air needed to cure North Carolina "bright leaf" tobacco. The barn in the foreground at right has large board shingles for roofing. The one at left has had its roofing material salvaged for another use.

BRAND NEW...AND CONDEMNED—Walter Nelson's son, Fred, had just moved his family into this new cottage on his father's farm when a government agent arrived with the news that the property was to become part of a new Marine Corps air station. The smokehouse in the backyard was designed to cure ham and other meat, a common process in the South before the advent of refrigeration.

MORE TYPICAL of the construction methods and conditions coming out of the economic depression of the 1930s was the Henry Richards homeplace which sported several rough-hewn additions. The Richards's 19 acres were located at Little Witness with its house on Shop Branch, a tributary of Hancock Creek.

THE WILL BERRY HOME, like many others, had been abandoned for months before documentary photographs were made under government contract. Berry owned eight acres in the Nelsontown community in the middle of what is today the Cherry Point Marine Corps Air Station. The unpainted plank-side house had a tar-paper roof, shutters for windows and a home-built front door.

GIVEN THE ERA, the Lucy Fisher home was a well-made structure of two-stories. Its massive brick chimney provided fireplaces and blessed warmth on both floors. The kitchen wing can be seen at rear. Fisher's home was on five acres at Nelsontown not far from Slocum Creek. Though the door and windows had been removed, the old white rose bush in the front yard continued to show off its blooms in the vacant structure's front yard.

CLEARLY WORSE FOR WEAR after its abandonment, the modest home of the Moses Sykes family was overgrown and stripped bare before the federal bulldozers rolled in to clear the land. The home was the center of a 19-acre farm at Nelsontown, one of the larger settlements on what is now Cherry Point. About five dozen families called Cherry Point home in the late 1930s.

THE HOUSE AND STABLES of Elizabeth West were on 17 acres at the center of the military base where huge jet runways intersect today. Nearly all of the displaced families found work and a much improved livelihood thanks to base construction and Civil Service employment. West's grandson, Alvin, however, grew up to be a teacher and later served as principal of Havelock's Tucker Creek Elementary School.

Chapter 2

A FAMILY ALBUM

PIONEERS—Taken circa 1890, the family portrait above shows some early and influential residents of Havelock. From left, Collins Hughes Hunter holding infant daughter Mary sits beside his wife, Betty Dudley Hunter. Collins was Havelock's postmaster in the 1880s. At right, Collins's father, James Howard Hunter, born in 1824, sports his finest duds and a handsome cane. Big Jim Hunter was a Civil War veteran who served as a Confederate officer and scout. He was one of the area's largest landowners with more than 500 acres on Slocum Creek. The elder Hunter made his living in naval stores, timber and farming. Well-known and respected, he was one of the county's wealthiest men and served as a magistrate and school board leader. He was often mentioned in the newspaper, sometimes just for visiting New Bern by train. He was later the overseer at the nearby Lake Ellis Plantation, a massive farm off Lake Road owned by James Augustus Bryan.

HAVELOCK BORN—Portrait of Collins Hunter as a younger man. Born during the Civil War at Havelock in 1863, Hunter would be postmaster in 1887. Early in life he was a seaman, but later worked for the railroad and then ran a country store. Late in life, Collins followed the railroad to Roxboro, N.C.

LIFELONG RESIDENT—John Noe Hunter, Collins's brother, was born at Havelock in 1859; one of four children of Jim Hunter and his first wife, Mary Jane Noe Hunter. At his death in 1905, John was buried on family land that today is at the center of Cherry Point. His headstone still stands at one of the many old cemeteries preserved on the base.

HIGH SOCIETY—After the death of two wives with whom he had eight children, Jim Hunter married Caroline Hardison of Croatan in 1881. Hunter was a successful businessman and farmer, and was prominent socially and politically. In his old age, he went to live with the family of his son, Collins, in Roxboro. There he died in 1920.

ELOPED—Mary Elizabeth Hunter, was born at Havelock in 1864 and one of the children of Jim Hunter's first marriage. Young "Betty" used a ladder to climb out of the second-story window of the family's Slocum Creek home on what is now Cherry Point to elope with Benjamin Williams, a much older neighbor described by the family as "nothing but a poor dirt farmer." The pair made their happy home near Croatan and raised six children.

SELF-MADE — Benjamin Etheridge Williams of Slocum Creek might have been poor when he married 19-year-old Betty Hunter in 1883, but he would not stay that way. Very religious and well-liked, Williams soon started a sugar cane grinding business that brought his family to prosperity. He would later serve on the school board and as a magistrate with his father-in-law, Jim Hunter.

WILLIAMS HOME—We don't know who these folks are, but they are posed in front of the Benjamin Williams home near Croatan. Ben and Betty's house was two-stories, plank-sided and devoid of paint, a typical farm home of the period. Note the "laundry room" at left.

Chapter 3
OLD HAVELOCK

MAINSTAY FAMILY—Edward D. Russell was the head of a big family that populated Havelock for generations. He was a farmer who served as magistrate and was the Havelock postmaster from 1881 to 1898. His family home was just west of the Atlantic and East Carolina railroad tracks on what is now Greenfield Heights Blvd. Pictured here with his second wife, Rebecca Jane Garner Russell, he is flanked by a son, Richard, and daughter, Sallie. Rebecca is holding Edward's granddaughter from his first marriage, Zippiette Armstrong. Edward Russell died of smallpox in 1902 not long after this portrait was made.

NURSE-MIDWIFE—The lovely woman, at right above, is Martha Lena Russell Armstrong of Havelock. Mattie was the daughter of Edward D. Russell and born in 1882 to his first wife, Sarah Meadows Russell. Mattie grew up at the intersection of the old dirt road from New Bern to Beaufort—today called Greenfield Heights Boulevard and Miller Boulevard—at the point where it crossed the Atlantic & East Carolina Railroad tracks. She married Earnest Alonzo Armstrong, a native of Maryland, who would later disappear amid mysterious circumstances. Together they raised seven children, including the three daughters, from left to right, Thelma, Eloise and Zippiette, posing above in their finest home-sewn dresses. For many years in the early 1900s the Armstrongs owned a two-story general store, stables and a "kitchen," or early restaurant, near the current location of Trader's Store which the Armstrong's businesses predated. Most important to the community, Mattie Russell provided the only immediate medical care for many decades and was considered to be the local "doctor." She delivered nearly all the babies, black and white, sat up with the sick and ministered to the critically injured or ill until the nearest licensed doctor could be fetched—from Newport. Folk medicines used in the early 1900s included sugar, kerosene and turpentine. Mattie Armstrong died in 1953 and is buried at the First United Methodist Church cemetery.

BEAR HUNT 1909 are the words scrawled on this photograph. Here two men sit between a campfire and a canvas lean-to as three others flank a small black bear hanging from a tree. Visible in the full image, supported by the tent's ridge pole, are an ammo belt, some small game and a double-barrel shotgun. Hunting was a way of life and such outdoor scenes were much more common a hundred years ago before the advent of automobiles, television, refrigeration, supermarkets and central heating.

HOME SWEET HOME—Havelock resident Ed White stands against his picket fence with wife, Elizabeth Pate White, and a loyal hunting dog in this 1898 scene. White has removed his straw hat for the photo made in front of his home on a stretch of the Beaufort Road now known as Miller Blvd. Today, the vacant White homesite lies between the Trader House and the Havelock Methodist Church.

ROUGH TO BE A BEAR—Another portrait of Ed White shows that he knew his way around the local woods. Dressed in a slouch hat and knee boots, White is armed with the long gun with which he killed a substantial bear in the forest near Havelock. In later life, White moved to New Bern to be closer to relatives. There he lived in a house on Hancock Street.

SLOCUM CREEK 1890—This amazing image shows a wooden bridge that once spanned Slocum Creek. In the foreground a man stands beside an oxcart while a two-horse wagon comes over the bridge. The exact location of the 1890 bridge is unknown, but it was probably in the vicinity of a small bridge that now crosses the creek on Greenfield Heights Blvd.

LAKE ROAD 1890—A hunting dog stands near the edge of what was known in the late 1800s as the Canal Road. Horsemen are approaching toward the viewer in the image as workers plow a field at left. A big canal once ran between Ellis Lake Plantation, now roughly the location of Camp Bryan, ending at Slocum Creek. The canal drained the lakes so more crops could be planted.

QUARTERS at Lake Ellis Plantation housed sharecroppers and farm laborers after the Civil War and later served as temporary housing for some of the many visitors who came from all over the East Coast to hunt and fish at Havelock. This image was made in the late 1800s. The plantation occupied thousands of acres and was located out Lake Road a few miles from the current city boundary.

OUT STANDING IN HIS FIELD—A single individual is visible in this view of a Lake Ellis Plantation farm field. The man is unidentified, but since James H. Hunter of Havelock was the well-known manager or "overseer" of the plantation during this period, it is not beyond reason to guess that he might have been the person photographed on the land owned by multi-millionaire James Augustus Bryan. Of course, it could just as easily be one of the many field hands who worked there.

LANDING OF THE TROOPS

CIVIL WAR INVASION—Havelock's Slocum Creek was the site of a massive federal amphibious landing on the morning of March 13, 1862 by a force of at least 11,000 Union soldiers bent on the capture of everything from New Bern to Beaufort. After preparatory artillery shelling, about sixty U.S. Navy ships disgorged the troops in the rain on beaches near present-day Carolina Pines not far from the location of the current Cherry Point officers club. This illustration appeared at the time in *Harper's Weekly*.

Block hous

HAVELOCK FORT—Federal troops built a "blockhouse," a log fort on the banks of Slocum Creek in Havelock in early 1862. Rotating Yankee companies of about one hundred men occupied the site to protect the vital railroad line until the fort was burned in an 1864 Confederate raid. The 1863 drawing by Union Pvt. Herbert Valentine shows the blockhouse at the Slocum Creek railroad trestle. To its left are officers' quarters and troop tents. The drawing, from the Southern Historical Collection at UNC Chapel Hill, was used as a guide for the creation of a Civil War diorama on display at the Havelock History Exhibit in the local Tourist and Events Center.

TURPENTINE STILL—For over a hundred years, the synthesis of pine tree sap into "naval stores" was a key to the local economy. Naval stores are tar, pitch, turpentine and other products used to build and maintain wooden ships. The huge turpentine distillery pictured here is typical of many such facilities that once dotted the local woods bringing both employment and wealth. Two men in the picture, at center and right, show the scale of the operation.

"GATHERING TURPENTINE" was the common name of the industry that began with slashes in a pine tree's bark causing sap to ooze out. Workers collected the thick, sticky sap for delivery to turpentine stills where it was processed by distillation. One of several techniques for tapping trees is shown here. The lucrative business waned in the last half of the 1800s with the Civil War and the advent of metal-hulled ships. Many families then left the Havelock woods for opportunity elsewhere.

LIQUOR STILL—Compare this Havelock moonshine still with the turpentine still on the opposite page and it's easy to see that one is simply a miniature version of the other. People of Havelock and nearby Harlowe, impoverished by the devastation of war and the collapse of the naval store business, turned to bootlegging, using proven distillation technology as a way to support their families. Liquor stills became common. Many took pride in their work. Here, S.M. "Sap" Hardy tends one in the woods near Gray Road.

REVENUERS—The bane of the moonshiner's life was lawmen like the three above who raided a still site near Havelock. Boxes in which corn mash fermented prior to distillation are seen at left and center and a brick-faced boiler is at right. Law enforcement officers like Norman Lee, Sr. of Havelock, at left above, and J.K. Clay, right, used axes and dynamite to put illegal liquor operations out of business. After the construction of Cherry Point, base pilots aided law officers by scouting area forests with helicopters. Good jobs at the base also resulted in many bootleggers leaving the trade.

OLD DEPOT—A portion of an 1890s-era Havelock railroad depot is seen at left in this view looking out Lake Road. Railroad tracks and a loading platform are visible in the foreground and corn is growing behind the white rail fence at right. A blow-up of the photo reveals a group of people walking on the road toward the viewer.

STORE AND DEPOT—A newer, fancier Havelock railroad depot is at right in this photo from about 1916. At center is the two-story Armstrong General Store with residence above and a kitchen and stable at rear. The location of the store is almost identical to that of the current Trader's Store. This view is to the east up what is now Miller Blvd. toward the current main gate of Cherry Point.

EAGLE EYE—Hunting near the Havelock area lakes, G.A. Nicholls had quite a day on January 23, 1910. According to information on the photo, he shot sixty-five ducks and two gobblers during the outing. After the hunt, he posed with turkeys in hand and his shot gun and apparently exhausted dog at his side. A few of the ducks were hung up to form a backdrop for the portrait.

A CANOE was a handy way to move around on the network of canals constructed to drain the Camp Bryan area. Here, H.H. Brimley navigates a waterway in search of wildlife.

GATOR HUNTERS—Herbert Hutchinsion Brimley, at right, knee-deep in a Havelock swamp with Dave Samson about 1911. Dave, born a slave near Havelock, accompanied Brimley on his many area hunts. Here, Dave carries a shovel and long hooked pole while Brimley packs substantial fire power in the form of a shoulder-slung rifle.

Brim - The Coon Hunter
Prince of Sportsmen

IN ALL HIS GLORY—H. H. Brimley poses before a Camp Bryan cabin with his latest trophy, a raccoon. A self-taught zoologist and taxidermist, Brimley gathered many of the specimens here that became the core collection of the N.C. Museum of Natural History in Raleigh which he founded with his brother, Clement. Brimley was born in England in 1861 and came to the U.S when he was nineteen.

AT CAMP BRYAN—Dave Samson, at left in apron and chef's hat, holds a few birds while Ben, a caretaker, holds a raccoon in one hand and the reins of a mule cart in the other. The photo was made shortly after New Year's 1911.

THE WELL-TO-DO—The Havelock area was a haven for wealthy businessmen and sports figures during the decades around 1900. New Yorkers were particularly fond of the hunting, fishing, and isolation plus maybe a nip or two of the famous Craven County corn liquor said to be plentiful hereabouts.

TO HAVELOCK—Atlantic and East Carolina Railroad trains passed through Havelock twice daily and advertisements boasted that the destination was less than twenty-four hours from New York and Philadelphia. This steam locomotive crossing the Trent River at New Bern is pulling two freight and two passenger cars.

THE HOT DOG KING—Frank Stevens, at right, is credited as the man who popularized the hot dog when he introduced it in 1902 at the Polo Grounds in New York City. Stevens, who also added popcorn and peanuts as standard fare at sporting events, loved spending time off at Havelock. The family concession business he created sold for $150 million in the 1960s.

HUNTING PALS—George Herman "Babe" Ruth came here so often half the families in town claimed close personal relations with the New York Yankee's legend. The man to Ruth's left in this photo is identified as Bud Fisher, the well known San Francisco cartoonist who invented "Mutt and Jeff."

A CLASSIC—Trader's Store is the only remaining example of many old country stores that served the Havelock area. Today, fully restored, it is the prize possession of the Havelock Historical Preservation Society and is open to the public. Founded by Hugh Trader in 1924, the store was operated for decades by Trader and into the 1970s by his family.

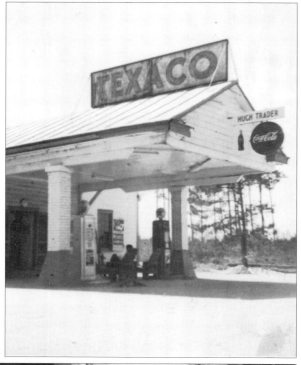

THE TRADERS—Elsie and Hugh Trader hold children, Sidberry and Cherry, on the back steps of their general store located on what is today Miller Blvd. If you couldn't find it at Trader's you probably didn't need it. Hugh is said to have eased many local families through the Great Depression by extending generous credit in those hard times.

HAVELOCK SCHOOL—By the time this photograph was made, wings and a porch had been added to the local one-room school house for use as a residence. The original shoe-box shaped structure, heated by a pot-belly stove, served as the community's center of elementary education for decades beginning just after 1900.

OLD SCHOOL—Another view of the one-room school house shows its location by the railroad tracks at the corner of Greenfield Heights Blvd. and Lake Road. When it was a school, the building was at the head of Gray Road on land that is now part of Indian Hills.

CLASS OF 1922-23—Teachers Rosalie Wynne, at left, and Annie Franks Reel, at right, watch over their students in front of the old Havelock schoolhouse. Among the group are children with family names Wynne, Ketner, Garner, Armstrong, Jackson, Muse, Hill, Bryan and others.

LAST DAY—In 1983, the owner of the building that had formerly been the old Havelock schoolhouse offered to donate the building, if it could be moved. The historic preservation effort failed, however, and the structure was burned as part of a local fire department training exercise.

BLACK SCHOOL—The one room school for Havelock's African-American students was built at the same time as the old white school featured above—about 1903—and was nearly identical in design and size. This one still existed in 2010 on private property along Greenfield Heights Blvd.

DON'T TRY THIS TODAY— In the 1930s, local gal Greta Oliver struck a coy pose in the middle of Highway 70. For many years, there was little to no traffic here. After the construction of the air base, Havelock experienced two brief daily periods of "base traffic" five days a week. Later came Friday night and Sunday afternoon summertime "beach traffic." Today, traffic-jammed US 70 absorbs several hundred thousand trips per week.

SOMETHING HIDDEN—A vintage automobile sits in front of Trader's Store in this late 1920s photo. Visible at right is today's Miller Blvd. and Church Road, then known as Central Highway 10 and later as U.S. 70. At left, is today's Miller Blvd. headed west out toward Greenfield Heights. The white spot in the circle is an old church that no longer exists. See photo below.

HAVELOCK CHRISTIAN—About fifty members of the Havelock Christian Church, including some sitting on a window sill, gathered for a photograph in the early 1900s. The church, which no longer exists, was located near a current entrance to Indian Hills. A blow-up of the photo reveals the robed minister in front of the open door at the center of the group. One of the children is said to be Zippiette Armstrong.

Chapter 4
OLD CHERRY POINT

OLD CHERRY POINT—The tiny settlement took the name Cherry Point Landing from a Neuse River promontory called Cherry Point to the east of adjacent Hancock Creek. The hamlet blossomed on the western side of the creek's intersection with the mighty Neuse and the name was shortened to Cherry Point when a post office opened there in 1890. Populated by people named Russell, their relatives and friends, the community thrived for decades near where Cherry Point's Hancock boat docks are today. In addition to homes and seasonal hunting and fishing camps, it had its own store, post office, and a small cemetery which exists to this day. Here, a woman and six children gather beneath a sign announcing the riverfront neighborhood. Note the old car in the background.

RUSSELLS — Annie and George Russell were the stalwart leaders of the small Cherry Point community. Annie was the "postmistress" while "Captain George" hired out as a fishing guide and charter boat skipper for tourists and outdoorsmen from all over the country. On Sundays, George was known to haul a boatload upriver to New Bern to attend Catholic services there.

RUSSELL HOME—The wood frame home of George and Annie Breslin Russell, deep into what is today the military base, served dual duty as the local post office. A native of Ireland, Annie wielded the local postmark from 1907 to 1932. Cherry Point mail sacks were transferred to and from trains at the Havelock railroad station by horse and mule carts until autos came on the scene.

MR. RUSSELL—Careful in his dress, pipe-smoking George Russell wears both suspenders and a belt in this portrait from his later years. The son of Havelock magistrate and postmaster Edward D. Russell, George was born here in 1876 and died in 1936, one year after his wife, Annie. Both are buried in the community cemetery near Hancock Creek.

POPEYE?—Nope, that's Pet Russell decked out for sheer comfort in a captain's hat with rolled-up pants and rolled-down socks. A bantam chicken prowls the ground behind him.

PET AGAIN—Just to prove that he could dress up when he wanted, here's Pet Russell in stylish haberdashery at Cherry Point with his wife, Missouri, whose nickname was "Zoodie."

PET AND ZOODIE Russell's home at Cherry Point in the 1920s. "Pet" was Anthony Russell's nickname. Zoodie's maiden name was Hill.

PEACHES—Old-timer Barclay D. Borden stands by a fruit, tree on his Cherry Point land. Borden, a farmer, fisherman and life-long resident, served as postmaster from 1901-1907. Borden drowned in the Neuse in 1923. Like many other old families, Borden still has descendents in the Havelock area.

NESTLED beneath a live oak tree is one of the old cemeteries still on Cherry Point. Fifteen cemeteries have been identified there. Some of the deceased known to be buried on the air station were alive at the same time as George Washington and Thomas Jefferson. Settlement in the area began in the early 1700s.

LICHEN IT—A young woman identified on the old Cherry Point photograph as Thelma Armstrong is draped with both Spanish moss and a fellow named T. L. King. In addition to sprucing up attire, the locally-common moss was often used as decoration for parties and holidays. Despite the ID, though, Thelma's family members are not so sure it's her.

PICNIC—A table heavy with food and a big group of friends and family was all it took to have a grand time. A vintage automobile is visible along with kids posing underneath the serving table. George Russell is third from right in this 1920s-era image. A hopeful hound lurks at left.

ALL SMILES...AND EARS—A gaggle of Cherry Point kids, some in classic overalls, ham it up for the camera in front of an old canvas tent. Camp tents often served quite well as additional housing when an overflow crowd of guests and relatives descended for a visit.

HAPPY DOZEN—A group of Cherry Point children enjoy maybe the best swimming hole ever in Hancock Creek at the site of the present-day Hancock boat docks. Visible in the photo are some of the handmade rowing skiffs used for fishing, recreation and transportation. In the early 1900s, it's fair to say everybody had a boat of one kind or another. And not an engine in sight.

HORSEPLAY—The four amateur acrobats shown frolicking in Hancock Creek are, from top to bottom, Doc Hill, Fred Bryan, C.P. Ketner (peeping to the left) with Johnny Trader in front.

ROWBOAT—Strong, simple interior design and construction of common skiffs is seen in this picture of kids in the creek. With simple planks for seats, all rowboats had hand bailers to deal with slow, but constant leaks. A competent carpenter could build one of the boats in a matter of days.

LATEST FASHIONS—Three Cherry Point ladies and a gentleman model the latest in casual attire and swim wear circa 1925. With some pretty snazzy hats, too. And we must say: "Nice legs, there, buddy."

BOATS—Large powerboats like this were used for fishing and hauling freight. Boats of this type are reputed to have been used to transport illegal, but popular, corn liquor along local creeks and the river where it could be off-loaded to larger vessels for shipment up the East Coast.

GATOR—The dude in the suit holds a small alligator and a rifle on the deck of George Russell's Sea Dog. Russell, at left, served as a local buoy tender for many years and also took customers out to hunt and fish. Russell's generation finished off all the large reptiles here in the northern range of the American alligator. Gators made a strong resurgence after endangered species laws were enacted in the 1960s.

BIG HATS—Well-shaded on the Neuse River shore at Cherry Point, these ladies have a crab net, loyal dog and toes in the water. Who needs more?

BIG FISH—When the prize requires a pole and two men to hold it up, it's been a good day of fishing. This channel bass, or puppy drum, will make a fine meal. But what about cleaning it?

THE ANSWER at the time was finding the right woman. Here, Annie Russell shows the boys a thing or two about preparing a seafood dinner.

NICE CATCH—But the grown men weren't the only ones who could fish as evidenced by this young fellow's haul of two fine largemouth bass. Amazing what you can do with a cane pole and a worm.

DINNER?—Look at the size of these turtles. Local people liked the meat and the soup that could be made from the big creatures. Someone thought the catch was worth a photograph, but did Cherry Point folks really turtle hunt in ties? Just asking.

OFF-ROADING—One of the men on the vehicle in the photo is Pet Russell. He and a buddy have just bagged some wild turkeys. The mud on the tires of the classic automobile raises yet another question: Did they shoot 'em from the car?

MORE TURKEYS—George Russell, at right, stands with a group of happy hunters who have just reduced the local turkey population. Turkeys, quail and dove along with deer, rabbits and squirrels augmented the diets of area residents who settled Cherry Point.

AND HOW did they get those turkeys cleaned and on the table? Look no further than the Russell women pictured here posing with the birds. Missouri and Helen Russell look capable, even if not one hundred percent thrilled.

Chapter 5

SEND IN THE MARINES

Marine Air Base, Cherry Point, N.C. Sept. 7, 1941. A part of reservation under construction looking N.E. Contract. 4957.

BASE CONSTRUCTION BEGINS—This remarkable aerial photograph from September 7, 1941 shows the state of construction at what would become the massive Cherry Point Marine Corps Air Station. The image was made two months to the day before the Japanese bombed Pearl Harbor, Hawaii on Dec. 7, 1941; a sneak attack that marked the beginning of the Second World War and put Cherry Point construction into overdrive. Eight thousand workers soon hustled to move ten million cubic yards of dirt, lay twenty-three miles of drainage pipe, plumb twenty-six miles of water line and connect twenty-five miles of electrical lines. None of the buildings shown along Highway 101, now known as Fontana Blvd., exist today although the one at extreme left survived at the location into the 1970s. The position of the current Main Gate is marked with an X. Gate Six at Cunningham Road is to the right. The 1941 route of Highway 70 arcs at the bottom of the photo. Visible at the top of the photo is the beginning of a runway. By the time the first planes landed, six months after this photograph was made, enough runway concrete had been poured to build a twenty-foot wide road from Havelock to Richmond, Virginia…with twenty-five miles left over.

OUT OF FORESTS AND FARMS would come "one of the most colossal building programs" of World War II, as a historian later said. Construction of Cherry Point's massive runways, big enough today to handle the Space Shuttle, is visible at the top of the photograph. Thousands of acres of forest were cleared. Much of the initial work was done—believe it not—with dynamite. The white spots visible in the foreground are craters where trees have been blasted. Much of the initial ditching was done the same way.

TRAINS BUILT THE BASE—Most of the endless material and 20,000 people that made up the base came on the wheels of Atlantic and East Carolina railroad steam trains like this one at the Havelock depot in 1944. Among many other things, one report says that the railroad brought 32,000 carloads of sand, much of it used in concrete, in a single year, 1942. The location of the railroad was a major reason Cherry Point was built at Havelock instead of the initially-selected site across the river in Pamlico County.

"THIS IS IT" is both a question and a statement of despair on the cover of a rare World War II comic book by Franklin R. Jones showing servicemen arriving by rail at Cherry Point. Two Marines in the first windows are accompanied by a sailor in back as they ride the sluggish "caterpillar" train to the desolate location marked by a crude directional sign watched over by a turkey vulture on a dead tree. A pipe-smoking railroad man with oil can stands idly by waiting to service the train.

THEY BUILT THE BASE—Four Navy engineers arrived in eastern North Carolina July 28, 1941 charged with overseeing the creation of a Marine base on an 11,000-acre patch of forest, swamps and farms. From left, Lt. Commander E.W.C. Nice and his team of three Navy lieutenants, William F. Merritt, William M. Gustafson, and J.K. Flynn, made the best hotel in the area, the Queen Anne in New Bern, their headquarters until a temporary administration building was completed at Cherry Point two months later. The Navy engineers coordinated the multiple construction firms, thousands of workers and myriad details necessary to complete the world's largest Marine Corps air station in less than three years. Close behind the Navy builders came Cherry Point's first Marine command: Lt. Col. Thomas J. Cushman, below right, and four enlisted men. A Missouri native, Cushman joined the Marines in 1917 and became an aviator the following year. None of it would have happened, however, without the efforts of Congressman Graham A. Barden of New Bern, below left, who seized the opportunity to procure the base for Craven County.

Congressman Barden   **Lt. Col. Cushman**

HANGAR CONSTRUCTION—Vintage aircraft and automobiles are in the foreground of a shot of one of Cherry Point's immense hangars as a crane, at left, lifts steel roof trusses into place. A train of fuel cars can be seen at the tree line, top left, while a dozen early helicopters dot the tarmac at top right. More than 4,000 structures of every imaginable type were built during the first thirty-six months of base construction.

HEADQUARTERS—Building 198 was one of Cherry Point's original structures built during World War II. The Headquarters Building, also called the Administration Building, or just "Admin" for short, is shown here as it appeared on a postcard in the late 1940s. The offices of the commanders of both the air station and the Second Marine Air Wing were in the C Street structure from the beginnings of the base until the building was damaged beyond repair by a massive fire September 8-9, 2007.

SQUADRON WENT TO WAR IN TRAILER—When found, the handwritten note paper-clipped to this old print read: *Photo of VMF(N)531 MAG-53 being hooked up to Cletrac for loading aboard train and further transfer overseas in April 1943.* The initial question was: How could a Marine squadron fit in a tiny trailer? A lot of research later, the story became clear. At the moment the trailer was being hooked to the strange Cletrac tractor, VMF(N)531 was in the process of becoming the Marine Corps's first night fighter squadron. With a grand total of two pilots and two North American SNJ-4 Texan aircraft (like the one pictured here), 531 headed to the South Pacific where its flyers became the first Marine or Navy night fighter squadron to operate against the Japanese. It was also the first U.S. squadron to fly on instruments at night and engage the enemy with the new RADAR technology received by American forces from the British in 1942. As VMFA-531 the squadron would later distinguish itself again flying F7F Tigercats in Korea, F-4 Phantom jets in Vietnam (where it became the first to fire Sparrow missiles) and the F-18 Hornet in the Gulf War. The famous Grey Ghosts, who began life at Cherry Point and went to war in a trailer on a train, were decommissioned in 1992 after fifty years of exemplary service.

HUMBLE START—Just two planes, like this restored SNJ-4 Texan, made up the total strength of VMF(N)531 when it went to war. (The "N" was the new designator for "night-fighter"). The squadron was later beefed-up with a few reclaimed Dutch SB2A-4 Brewster Buccaneer dive bombers. The unit's pilots would one day fly the most sophisticated aircraft in the U.S. arsenal.

A REGIMENTAL REVIEW, Third Marine Aircraft Wing on December 11, 1943 included, front row left to right: Brigadier General Claude A. Larkin, Wing CG; Colonel Carl S. Day, CO OTS-8; Col. C.F. Schilt, Air Station CO; and Capt. K.D. Lynch, CO Women's Reserve Squadron 45. Back row: Col. Pierson Conradt, Col. Frank M. June, LtCol. O.E. Bartoe, LtCol. W.J. Huffman and others at attention on a barely grassed Cherry Point parade ground with vintage autos in the background.

THE BOYS—This World War II image of Marines and sailors posed on a Jeep at Cherry Point shows clearly the youth and innocence of the thousands of beloved servicemen who saved America by fighting from 1941-1945. Look at those faces and no other words are necessary.

CLOWNING FOR THE CAMERA—Some of Cherry Point's temporary quarters are visible in this shot from the early 1940s. The square huts with fold-up window covers each had a heater at the center and low-slung electrical wires held up by a wooden mast. Housing was one of the biggest challenges during the early days as the population of the base swelled to 20,000. Here, young servicemen pose with two of the military's most essential pieces of equipment in that era: a Jeep and a mop.

C-130 PRECURSORS—Two of the classic aircraft of Cherry Point's history are the R4D "Gooneybird" transport in the foreground being pulled by a tractor and an R4Q with its distinctive twin tail fins at rear. Both aircraft hauled people and cargo around the world for decades of reliable service spanning World War II and Korea.

AIRBORNE—The R4Q "Flying Boxcar" was once a common sight in the skies of Craven County. Cherry Point's VMGR-252 flew the Boxcars designed to carry personnel, material, medical cases, and mechanized equipment and also to deliver troops or cargo by parachute. First flown in November, 1947, the Fairchild Aircraft Company ceased production of the plane in 1955, but it continued to serve the Marine Corps until the C-130 was introduced in 1961.

AIR TRAFFIC CONTROL, the old fashioned way. Cherry Point gunnery range officers keep watch from the top of an ordnance shack during an aerial gunner refresher course. The men checked for firing accuracy, made sure the tow planes were on course and kept a lookout for fishing boats. From left, WO H.M. Carris, Rochester, VT.; T/Sgt Kirkpatrick McCord, Kingsville, TX.; M/Sgt Ernest Foltz, Auburn IN.; and S/Sgt Roland Staffieri, Bronx. NY; use the basics to do the job: binoculars, a mike and Ray-Bans.

HIGH TECH MESSAGING—The latest technology in communications during the early days was the Cherry Point Western Union telegraph office. Staffed by fourteen enlisted Women Marines and one civilian, Jewel Griffin, shown here at right operating a teletype machine, the telegraph office whizzed a heavy volume of messages around the world.

CELEBRITIES—A number of famous people have served at Cherry Point. At left, world heavyweight boxing champion Joe Louis, a Marine sergeant, put on exhibition bouts here in 1945. Popular movie star, First Lt. Tyrone Powers, right, was a transport pilot here in 1944. Baseball slugger Ted Williams flew the Grumman F9F Panther at Cherry Point in 1952.

GOVERNOR VISITS—North Carolina Governor Kerr Scott reviewed the troops at Cherry Point during an official visit in 1950. Maj. Gen. L. E. Wood, Second Marine Air Wing commander, is visible over Scott's shoulder. Scott was particularly interested in economic development and recognized the military base as a boon to the quality of life in eastern Carolina. Under the Scott administration (1949-1958) much of the state's roadways were paved and highways built.

ACE OF A FELLOW—One of the Marines who contributed to Havelock's growth was Paul John Fontana (1911-1997). Joining the Marine Corps in 1936, Fontana became an aviator in 1940. He gained acclaim as a great leader and aerial combat ace during World War II. By the time Major General Fontana retired in 1973, he'd fought in Korea and Vietnam, earned a hero's collection of medals and held the top three commands at Cherry Point: the station, the wing and the aviation depot. He and wife Beth raised their children here, making their home at Carolina Pines. The city showed its respect and affection in 1993, naming the street bordering the base "Fontana Boulevard" in his honor.

WOMAN'S WORK during World War II included just about everything a man could do. Women worked in factories, flew aircraft everywhere but in combat, were the backbone of the medical services, and took any job possible to free up men for the fighting front. Here, a Woman Marine at Cherry Point prepares her camera for an aerial photography mission in the 1940s.

THE WORKHORSE—A Marine C-130 tanker gives a sip to a couple of thirsty fast-movers above eastern North Carolina. Since the 1960s, the versatile aircraft has played major roles for the Marine Corps. In addition to in-flight refueling, the mighty Hercules transports troops and equipment, make parachute drops, hauls the sick and wounded and serves as a weapons firing platform and more. The A-4 Skyhawks trailing the tanker used to be as common as clouds in the skies over Cherry Point. The small, agile attack jets first saw service in the 1950s, but were finally retire in the 1990s.

HOUSING SHORTAGE—When the population zoomed from a few hundred to 18,000 in ten years, housing was at a premium in Havelock. One solution was the numerous trailer parks, like one behind Hall's Radio & TV, 328 E. Main Street, that sprang up like summer flowers. Lacking full bathrooms, mobile home residents of the late 1940s shared communal bath houses. It was something like camping, but better than conditions for people living in attics or two fellows we heard of who roosted for a while in a chicken coop.

TYPICAL LOCAL HOUSING—With no air conditioning, a porch sheltered by a canvas awning was a nice amenity for military and civilian families making the best of trailer park life in the late 1940s and early 1950s. Lacking infrastructure and skilled labor it took several decades for housing supply to match demand.

TYPICAL LOCAL FAMILY—Janice Forrest Ellis, who grew up on the Neuse River between New Bern and Havelock, stands by her Navy corpsman husband, Ed, in front of their Hall's Trailer Park home off East Main Street. Ed, a native of Goldsboro who went on to a life-long career at Cherry Point, holds the couple's son, the future author of this book, on a warm summer day in 1951.

HOUSING SOLUTION—When little local initiative developed to meet residential demand, several massive federal building projects got underway aboard the air station. Here, the brand new "Staff Capehart" housing area is seen from the air at the time of its completion in the 1960s. The uniform, mostly three-bedroom, ranch houses sported carports facing neatly laid-out streets. Cherry Point's "industrial area" and runways are visible at the top of photo.

OFFICER COUNTRY—The career was demanding, stressful and sometimes dangerous, but the view from home was magnificent. Here, newly completed Marine officer housing lines the miles-wide Neuse River. Hundreds of "housing units" built at Cherry Point in the 1950s and 1960s helped ease the residential crunch until local builders began to create new subdivisions in and around Havelock.

Chapter 6

A MODERN BOOM TOWN

MARINE CORPS 1959—Spurred by the growth of the Cherry Point Marine Corps Air Station, the tiny railroad hamlet of Havelock boomed in the 1940s. By 1959, it was the Town of Havelock with its own government, incorporated by the State of North Carolina. The photograph above shows some of the latest U.S. Marine Corps weapons in the year the town charter was enacted. The rifleman at left is outfitted with the era's standard combat gear including the M14, a caliber 7.62mm weapon that would stay in the inventory until replaced by the M16. At right, an ONTOS tank killer threatens with its six barrels. "The Thing," as it was nicknamed, would later see action against ground forces in Vietnam. Hovering above is the YRON-1 "Rotorcycle," an experimental design that saw little use and was retired in the 1960s. As Havelock and Cherry Point have grown together, the 2009 population approached 28,000 residents, a virtual dead heat with the county seat of New Bern.

PUBLISHER—Many in the civilian community played a role, but Charles H. Markey is representative of local business leaders since the 1950s. Markey Advertising published an early "shopper" newspaper, *The Markey Mailer*, along with area maps, local guide books and other products. Charlie was a long-time booster of all things Havelock, a veteran volunteer and a collector of local history and legend.

RESTAURATEUR—Joe Stewart shows off a classic pizza pie in the kitchen of the Italian Chef, a Main Street dining destination for thirty years following its opening in 1959. Stewart oversaw a kitchen specializing in spaghetti, lasagna, pizza and many other dishes loved by loyal customers, while wife Sylvana, a native of Italy, ran the dining room and general business operation.

CLOTHIER—The Men's Shop catered to the sartorial needs of the gents, military and civilian, in the growing community. Owned and operated by Joseph Rachide, shown here inspecting a dress uniform, the shop was located in the Commercial Shopping Center on Cunningham Boulevard. Joe Rachide was an early leader and driving force in the Havelock Retail Merchants Association, a forerunner of the local chamber of commerce, which worked to promote both business growth and good relations with local military members.

TEEN CLUB—Quonset huts on Highway 101 served as the weekend evening venue for teenagers during the 1960s. Businessmen like Rachide, above, worked out the details for use of the base property. One of the huts offered sofas, chairs, jukebox and dance floor, while the other had a pool table and bathrooms. The teen club provided a safe place for the kids to enjoy each other's company and blow off a little steam.

DING HAO DRIVE-IN THEATER—Located on East Main Street where Elizabeth Street is today, the Ding Hao was the place to go to see your movie favorites of the 1950s from the comfort of your automobile. This aerial photo shows the drive-in operated by local legend Irving Beck. Charles Street and Vine Street are visible in the picture, as are Stewart's Pure Oil, at center, and the Rose Motel, left center.

ROADSIDE ACCOMMODATION—A picture of the Rose Motel on East Main Street shows the state of the industry in the late 1940s. Later called the Base Motel, the business operated for several decades before being converted into apartments. The building was still there in 2009.

TOWN LEADER—Irv Beck, with a snappy hat and pocket full of cigars, reviews a copy of the report on incorporation for the Town of Havelock. Beck was one of the town's founding commissioners when it was established in 1959. After his stint in the movie theater business, the Marine World War II veteran was a leading insurance broker and civic booster for the rest of his life.

DING HAO meant "the best," but that didn't make the place hurricane-proof. A strong 1958 storm destroyed the theater's screen bringing the end of an era. Ever the jokester, Beck put "No Feature Tonight" on the damaged marquee. After the decision was made not to re-open, he changed the letters to read, "Gone With the Wind."

NAMESAKE—Havelock's Little League field is named for William Anthony Kleschick, Jr., the founder of the local youth baseball league. His volunteer role is representative of the efforts of thousands of Marines and former Marines in the growth of Havelock. Above, Kleschick stands at left in the photograph with the O&R team he coached. (The former O&R, Overhaul & Repair, operated as the Fleet Readiness Center East in 2010.) Kleschick

William Kleschick

was born in Philadelphia in 1918, served with the Marines in South Pacific combat from 1941-44, and was honorably discharged as a master sergeant. While working at O&R, he organized the league, was its first president and held many of the first league meetings in his home with his wife serving refreshments. Kleschick died suddenly in October 1959, the year of the town's founding. The baseball field was soon named in his honor. Many of Havelock's children have gone on to successful lives and careers. The batboy at center of the front row in the team photo is the coach's son, Bill. Today, Dr. William Kleschick, Havelock High School Class of 1968, is Global Director of Discovery Research for Dow AgroSciences.

BIG DAY—Local leaders received the Havelock town charter on August 24, 1959 in a ceremony at N.C. Secretary of State Thad Eure's office in Raleigh. In the front row, from left, are Mayor George Griffin, Eure, and Havelock Commissioner Reuel Lee. Back row, from left, City Attorney Kennedy Ward, Commissioner Irv Beck, Commissioner Clay Wynne, and Havelock business representatives Ray Vawter and Dick Flye.

HUMBLE BEGINNINGS—The fledgling government began life in a small rental space on East Main Street, across the highway from where city hall is today. The first annual budget for the Town of Havelock was $2,500.

THE SECOND TOWN HALL is still the home of Havelock government today, although it has been expanded through the years. The building was originally a community chapel built to serve the needs of Cherry Point personnel. There, in the early days of the base, Protestant services would be held at one hour and Catholic services the next. Many young couples tied the marital knot here before the Town of Havelock acquired the building from the federal government.

THE WINNERS—The first town board is all smiles in an early session after winning the fight for local governance. From left, Commissioner Jesse Lewis, Commissioner Norwood Sanders, Commissioner Reuel Lee, Mayor George Griffin, Commissioner Clay Wynne and Commissioner Irv Beck.

FIRST TOWN CLERK—Fourth from the left in this photo is Ernie Marquez, who told the board he'd do anything he could to help the new town operate. Marquez was rewarded by being named town clerk, a post that required its occupant to deal with all the paperwork and accounting to run the government. Marquez worked diligently at his post for several years. His town salary? Zero dollars, zero cents. Others here are Lewis, Lee, Griffin, Wynne and Beck.

RIBBON CUTTING—Fourth from left, Havelock's first mayor, George Griffin, like all small town mayors, did a lot of officiating. Here he snips the red ribbon marking the grand opening of a brand new grocery store, the A&P, while store management looks on. Our favorite thing about this photo is that the gentleman at extreme left didn't get the memo that everyone would be wearing eyeglasses that day.

A HERO COMES TO HAVELOCK—It was indeed a red letter day when Marine astronaut Col. John Herschel Glenn, Jr. came to town. The Marine Corps fighter pilot was among NASA's first group of seven astronauts, the Mercury Program, and was the first American to orbit the earth in space. In his spacecraft, Friendship 7, Col. Glenn circled the planet three times on February 20, 1962 as the entire country held its breath and watched on live television. In December, 1963 Glenn visited Cherry Point where he began his military career. The astronaut made several stops in Havelock drawing big crowds all day. At left, Glenn is welcomed by Monsignor Frank Howard in front of Annunciation Catholic Church and school on East Main Street. Mayor Griffin is at extreme left and Havelock's town hall is visible between Glenn and Father Howard. Above, Glenn is enthusiatically greeted by beaming students at Graham A. Barden Elementary School on Cedar Drive.

HAVELOCK DEPOT—When the old Havelock freight depot was moved to a new location on Miller Blvd. in January 2006, the date August 20, 1941 was found etched in its concrete foundation. The inscription marked another relocation of the building; this one from Riverdale to Havelock at the beginning of construction of the local Marine base. This image is the depot at its original trackside location at the intersection of Miller Blvd. and Lake Road in the late 1950s.

DIESEL POWER—Southern Railway engine number 1044 idles at the Havelock station in the 1960s. Although hard to see here, just below the engine numbers are the letters A&EC. That "fallen flag" designator stood for Southern's predecessor, the Atlantic & East Carolina Railway. The A&EC, a short line that ran from Goldsboro to Beaufort, was one of the first railroads in the country to move from steam to one hundred percent diesel power.

ROSE MOTORS—The Robert L. Rose Ford dealership stood on Main Street near Roosevelt Blvd. where the Annunciation Church sanctuary is today. When Goldsboro businessman Rose decided to move the dealership, his nephew, Hubert Rose, opened a furniture store there. Annunciation later purchased the property for its expansion and Rose Brothers Furniture moved west toward Slocum Creek. Members of the Rose family still run what (along with Mel-Burn Cleaners and Cherry Cab) is one of Havelock's oldest continuously-operated businesses.

ANNUNCIATION—Havelock's Catholic Church still had a dirt parking lot at its 1954 dedication. Pictured here are the original school and church building at 246 East Main Street that opened in the same year with about 350 students. The original church building was replaced by a new one at the former Rose site in 1969. The old church building and school were demolished to make way for a new school and gym that opened in late 2007.

OLDEST CHURCH—Havelock's First United Methodist Church started its life of service in the 1880s making it the oldest continuously active church in town. Teams of oxen were used to drag the first timbers to the saw mill. Here, in an undated photo, the original church is readied for the building of additions still in use today.

THE BIG BRICK CHIMNEY of St. Timothy's Lutheran Church on Highway 70 West was intended to accommodate the building's first use: a barbecue restaurant. John Moore tried to no avail to duplicate his successful New Bern eatery here. In the long Havelock tradition of adaptation, the building was later found to be a useful layout for church services which began there in the same year as the city's incorporation, 1959.

THE CHERRY POINT SCHOOL was built in the 1940s to meet the educational needs of the children of military personnel and local civilian families. The public school was located on Cunningham Blvd. across from the Commercial Shopping Center and later saw life as Havelock Junior High and Havelock Elementary. It has since been demolished to make way for a new school on the same site.

FIRST SHOPPING CENTER—All the modern conveniences were available when the new stores of the Commercial Shopping Center opened their doors on Cunningham Blvd. in the late 1940s. The center boasted a grocery, a pharmacy, and the Cherry Theater where all the latest Hollywood features were shown. A studio built as a second floor on one end of the building housed the town's first radio station, WUSM.

COMPETITION—The Commercial Shopping Center was given a run for its money when the Slocum Shopping Center opened on Park Lane and Highway 70 in the 1950s. With a First Citizens bank, a Colonial Store supermarket, a pharmacy, a Sears and a Western Auto store, among others, Havelock's retail sector was on a roll.

GROCER FOR MAYOR—Bananas were nine cents a pound when this photo was snapped at Snipes Grocery on East Main Street near the intersection of Roosevelt Blvd. in the late 1950s. The owner of the small market, John Snipes, was one of three candidates for mayor of the fledgling Town of Havelock in 1959. The victor, George Griffin, edged out a retired Marine colonel, Zeb Hopkins, by only a few votes, and Snipes by a wider margin.

HAVELOCK HIGH—Until good ol' HHS opened its doors in the mid-1950s, Havelock high school kids had been bussed to New Bern schools for decades. The new school created the Havelock Rams, an eternal rival for that other city's sports teams. A Havelock High football coach was once quoted as saying that, although championships were nice, his real job was to beat the New Bern Bears. The building at 102 High School Drive today houses Havelock Middle School.

FIRST COUNTY BUILDING—Beginning in the 1950s, this squat, block building with the snappy awnings at the corner of Miller Blvd. and Park Lane housed three local government operations under one small roof. The Havelock Library, a sheriff's office and the driver's license bureau shared the space for several decades.

H&N CHEVROLET—As established as any business can be in a small town, H&N was an integral part of the business community for nearly fifty years. Located at the corner of West Main Street and Jackson Drive, H&N rode the crest of General Motors's success with such muscular vehicles as the Impala, Chevelle and Corvette. The showroom featured a huge stuffed grizzly bear shot by a family member and curiously, in the 1960s, became one of the first places in North Carolina to sell surfboards.

YE LOCAL BUTCHER—Butcher shops like Havelock Meat and Davis's Meat Market on East Main St. were the place for homemakers to go for the finest cuts and best selection until national franchise supermarkets swept in and took over that segment of the business. Butcher shops hark back to a simpler time, but were common in Havelock just like in every other city, large or small, up to the 1960s.

LOOKS LIKE A GUTTER BALL—The Crossroad Bowling Lanes were located at the town's main intersection where Burger King and KFC are today. The hang-out featured a snack bar and "soda fountain," pin-ball machines and a juke box. In other words, it had almost everything a teenager or young Marine needed for entertainment at the time. Check out all those crew-cuts.

DRIVE-IN—Places like the Quik "N" Tastee and the Jet Drive-in (of which we've never been able to find a picture) served up fast, inexpensive food at a time before companies like McDonald's came on the scene. These were places to eat, hang around, see and be seen. Teenagers being teenagers, the Quik "N" Tastee was nicknamed the "Quick & Nasty." It was located on Main Street where Papa John's Pizza was in 2010.

GONE, BUT NOT FORGOTTEN by older citizens are the days when a service station was a "service" station. No sooner had your car stopped at the pumps than a team of men would descend to check water, oil and tire pressure at no charge. At your request, they would fill your tank or give you "a dollar's worth" (about four gallons) while they washed your windshield. In those happy days, three or four bucks would fill the tank of the solid steel V-8 beasts of the road.

TEXACO STAR—Wynne Brothers Service Station on East Main was owned by Clay and W. J. Wynne, descendants of one of Havelock's pioneer families of the 1800s. The brothers were movers and shakers who pulled hard for the community after starting their working lives behind their father's farm plow in the center of what is today Havelock. Clay became a Havelock-founding town commissioner. W. J. was a county commissioner and a leader of rural electrification efforts.

Chapter 7
SIR HENRY HAVELOCK

AFTERMATH OF BATTLE—British General Henry Havelock (1795-1857), the white-haired gentleman to the left of the white horse at center, is greeted by other military leaders after the victory at the Battle of Lucknow in India, 1857. The end of the "Sepoy Mutiny," as the uprising is known to history, brought word to Havelock that he had been knighted by the Queen of England and promoted to the rank of major general. It was quite an advancement for a man passed over for promotion twenty-two times earlier in his military career. But the brilliance of his heroic victories, which included, at one point, sixteen battles in sixteen days, deserved no less. Four days after the meeting depicted here, Havelock, 62, would fall ill. In four more days, he would be dead. His untimely passing, so soon after his triumph, only strengthened his legend. For a moment in time, Havelock was the most famous man in the world. The aftermath of the fight for the central Indian city of Lucknow is captured in this panoramic oil painting hanging today in the British Museum in London. Major General Sir Henry Havelock is the center of the scene depicting the carnage and destruction of a war largely forgotten except in places named in his honor, like Havelock, North Carolina.

IDEALIZED—After the death of Sir Henry Havelock in 1857, there was world-wide demand for his likeness. This portrait is an imagined visage, one of hundreds that were produced of the fallen hero. Here, a youthful Havelock wears medals that were actually awarded posthumously. Havelock was born in England, died in India and never set foot in America.

TRUE IMAGE—The only photograph ever taken of Havelock was a tiny portrait worn in his wife's locket. Following his death, Lady Havelock allowed that portrait to be used for the engraving at left, the best image we have of the city's namesake. Lady Havelock was honored with a pension that kept the family well off for several generations. Havelock's son, also named Henry, served with him as a young officer in India. The son would also rise to the rank of major general and become a Member of Parliament as well.

LEADING FROM THE SADDLE—Battle images of Havelock often show him in the thick of the fight to save British men, women and children during a bloody revolt in India. With brilliant tactics and poise under fire, he led his forces to several victories in fights where they were outnumbered five to one. Dozens of rare biographies of Havelock and accounts of the Sepoy Mutiny of 1857, donated by the author, are held in the Special Collections Library at East Carolina University in Greenville.

WAR HERO—A statue of Major General Sir Henry Havelock was raised in Trafalgar Square in the middle of London shortly after his death where it overlooks the city to this day. Three cities in the United States are named for him. Others include Havelocks in Iowa and Nebraska. There are two in Canada and two in New Zealand as well.

ACKNOWLEDGEMENTS

The author wished to thank and remember the many people, alive and deceased, who made this project possible.

Among those are Margaret and Cherry Trader, Harold and Linda Rawls, Ernie Buschhaus, Sandra Hardy, Thelma Norris, Charlie Markey, June Rodd, Jean Bryan, Jimmy Simmons, Diane Hodges, Michael Barton, Lila Wynne Simmons, Gary Nethercutt, George Griffin, Jack Murphy, Jim Beasley, Pat Bailey, Clay Wynne, John Green, Carmen Ellis, Arthur W. Edward, Dick Tuttle, Irv Beck, Chris Callahan, Dave Smith, Amanda Ohlensehlen, the Havelock 50th Anniversary Committee, the Havelock Historical Preservation Society, the Eastern Carolina Aviation Heritage Foundation, Mayor Jimmy Sanders and the Commissioners of the City of Havelock, the *Havelock News* and many others who have been helpful and generous over many years.

A tip of the hat and deep bow to Skip Crayton and Bill Benners of McBryde Publishing, New Bern, for valued and continuing support.

Very special thanks is in order to graphic artist Shannon Richards of Havelock who worked tirelessly with the author for many months in the book's layout and design.

And, as always, my wife and best ally, Veronica.

ABOUT THE AUTHOR

Eddie Ellis is Havelock's historian. He has been a student of Craven County's heritage since childhood. He spends much of his time reading, writing, researching and reporting about the area's past. This is his third book of local history.

The former newspaper professional founded the *Havelock News* in 1986 and was a long-time publisher of Cherry Point's *Windsock*. In partnership with his wife, Veronica, he is now a real estate developer.

The Ellises divide their time between homes in Raleigh and New Bern.

To contact Eddie Ellis: ebe@edwardellis.com.
For copies of the book, go to edwardellis.com

ISBN 978-0-9843184-1-4

$ 17.95

51795

9 780984 318414

McBryde Publishing